THE WINNING WORD

by
MICHAEL OSEI

Published by
Filament Publishing Ltd
16, Croydon Road
Beddington,
Croydon CR0 4PA
www.filamentpublishing.com
+44(0)20 8688 2598

© Michael Osei 2017
ISBN 978-1-912256-55-6

The right of Michael Osei to be identified as the author of this work has been asserted by him in accordance with the Designs and Copyrights Act 1988

All rights reserved
No portion of this work may be copies without the prior written permission of the publishers.

Printed by CreateSpace

Unless otherwise indicated, all scripture quotations in this book are from the New King James Version of the Bible.

Scripture taken from the New King James Version®. Copyright © 1982 by Thomas Nelson. Used by permission. All rights reserved.

Other scripture references are from the following sources:

THE HOLY BIBLE, NEW INTERNATIONAL VERSION®, NIV® Copyright © 1973, 1978, 1984, 2011 by Biblica, Inc.® Used by permission. All rights reserved worldwide.

Scripture is taken from GOD'S WORD®, © 1995 God's Word to the Nations. Used by permission of Baker Publishing Group.

Scripture quotations marked HCSB are taken from the Holman Christian Standard Bible®, Copyright © 1999, 2000, 2002, 2003, 2009 by Holman Bible Publishers. Used by permission. Holman Christian Standard Bible®, Holman CSB®, and HCSB® are federally registered trademarks of Holman Bible Publishers.

Easy to Read®, Copyright © 2006 by Bible League international.
World English Bible®, WEB.

Scripture quotations marked (NLT) are taken from the Holy Bible, New Living Translation, copyright © 1996, 2004, 2007 by Tyndale House Foundation. Used by permission of Tyndale House Publishers, Inc., Carol Stream, Illinois 60188. All rights reserved.

Acknowledgements

I want to thank God for making it possible for me to get this book out. I also want to thank my family especially my mum Victoria for bringing me up in the fear of God and for always supporting whatever I pursue. I also want to thank my sisters Debbie and Emmanuela for their love, encouragement and support. Words can't describe how much I love and appreciate you.

I want to thank the great men and women God has used to shape my life: Pastor and Mrs Raymond Odei (COP), Pastor and Mrs Emmanuel Danso (COP), Pastor and Mrs Dr. Ben Debrah (COP), Rev. and Mrs Charles Adupong (COP), Pastor and Mrs Dr. Ogonna Obudulu (Deeper Christian Life Ministry), Pastor and Mrs Delmar Asorwoe (COP), Elder and Mrs Nicholas Dapaa (COP), Elder and Mrs Robert Moore (COP), Dcns. Sarah Bonna (COP), Mr. Nfum and many others who have helped me in my walk with God.

I also want to thank Pastor Dr. Lord Elorm-Donkor for writing the foreword; Elder William Dankwa, Buyce Ampomah and Jessica Ansah

for their help during the entire process. This wouldn't have been possible without you.
I am very grateful to all my fellow workers at the Church of Pentecost - Archway District PIWC for your incredible love and support.

Last but not the least, I want to say a special thank you to all the youths at Archway District. You always support every project that I embark on. You challenge me to be a better Christian and youth leader. I bless God for your lives and you mean so much to me. The best is yet to come.

FOREWORD

We live in a fast-changing world where knowledge, skill and experience are highly prized. One's knowledge, skills and experience often put a value on that individual in society and in their jobs. The higher value one has determines his or her power for bargaining in occupational and social contexts. The desire to be valued above other people and to have more influence and acquire more material things has led us to be self-centred and self-promoting. As we focus on promoting ourselves we put God on reserve bench. Only a few people go to him when they are tired or lost track.

Consequently, we neither have peace nor genuine satisfaction of anything we have nor rest from our troubles because we are fighting our ways through life. However, the more we fight on, the more we realise that we cannot win on our own. But because we do not understand of our human condition, there are battles going on within ourselves, in all aspects of our lives, physically and spiritually and between other people and us. In this miserable condition how do can we survive, how can we win these various battles?

Michael Osei has the answer for us in this book. He has done both young and old people a great service by writing The Winning Word. This book identifies the war that we have in this world and guides the reader to find his or her ways through the many challenges using the God's word – the winning word. He explains how the winning word, as God's manual, is able to lead you through the battles of this life to become continuously victorious over every situation.

Michael indicates that by a constant and careful study and meditation on the word of God your faith will increase and you will know the will of God for your life and for all situations that confront you. Knowing the will of God gives you rest in the Lord and activates the manifestation of the power of God in your life in a way that makes you achieve great heights. The winning word gives you understanding of your new status in Christ. It is the solid foundation of your life, the rock on which every aspect of your life is built. Family, friends, job, wealth and fame are not permanent.

The only thing that remains forever is the word of God, the winning word.

Michael also explains in the book that to have the winning word, you must study the Bible because "to fail to prepare, is to prepare to fail". He clarifies that to do a good Bible study you must get a good Bible translation or a Bible app that is easy to understand and a notebook for writing down the insights the Holy Spirit gives you in your Bible study. Then you must pray consistently for the Holy Spirit to give you understanding of the winning word for every situation. You must be consistent in meditation and declaration while avoiding any distractions during your Bible study time. You must be obedient to the winning word of God for you to win.

This book is written in very straightforward language with glaring clarity for easy understanding. Michael Osei uses authentic biblical characters as examples to demonstrate that the word of God is able to change your status, circumstance and conditions in life and bring you to God's will. Similarly, in a very practical way, Michael uses his own testimonies to explain how it is possible that a failing student could become an excellent student by the use of the winning word.

There are very precious nuggets hidden on the following pages for anyone who desires to win in God's way. Therefore, I recommend this book unreservedly to every young believer. A careful reading and application of the truth in this book will guarantee your winning.

    Dr. Lord Elorm Donkor (Ph.D)
    Principal, Birmingham Christian College
    Birmingham, UK.

CONTENTS

Foreword   7

Preface   12

Introduction   15

Chapter 1
A new Kingdom   21

Chapter 2
God's manual for victorious living   25

Chapter 3
The benefits of God's word   39

Chapter 4
The Sure foundation   `57

Chapter 5
The Bible study session   83

Chapter 6
Obey the word   91

PREFACE

Right from Sunday school and especially when I hit my teenage years, we were always taught at church to read our Bibles and pray everyday, and even sang songs about it. This was all good but the older I got, the more I realised that many of the youths (including myself) didn't have a deep understanding of why we need to read our Bibles. One of the reasons was that when I asked an adult at church why I need to read my Bible, a typical answer I received was, "Because it's good for you." That was hardly inspiring. Although I knew that somehow the Bible is very important in my Christian journey, I didn't have a good understanding of exactly why I needed to make time and study it. I used to read my Bible just so I wouldn't feel guilty at church on Sunday.

Later, in my university years, my relationship with God deepened and I finally came to a better understanding of the benefits of studying the Bible. I came to learn that the Bible is a supernatural book and contains everything that I need to overcome the challenges that will come my way. I also understood that studying the Bible is a requirement to live a successful and fulfilling life.

I have been by privileged to preach the gospel of Jesus at churches, conferences and seminars in different parts of the UK. From my interactions with the people I've come across, many Christians, both young and old, are facing the same issues that I faced in my teenage years. They do not have an in-depth understanding of the benefits of studying the Bible. The only thing they seem to know is that when they die, they will go to heaven. Although this is true, the Bible makes it very clear that the blood of Jesus has made us Kings and Priests for us to reign on the earth.

And they sang a new song, saying:
> "You are worthy to take the scroll, And to open its seals; For You were slain, And have redeemed us to God by Your blood out of every tribe and tongue and people and nation, and have made us kings and priests to our God; And we shall reign on the earth." (Revelation 5:9-10)

We have been saved to reign on the earth. Jesus has bought us from the slavery of sin and has made us Kings and Priests (1 Peter 2:9). So, every believer has been made a king to rule on earth. This was the instruction that God gave the first human beings on earth, Adam and Eve. Although they lost their kingship authority to the devil because of sin, Jesus has defeated the devil and taken that authority from the devil and given it back to us, the believers. Jesus said that, All authority has been given to Me in heaven and on earth. (Matthew 28:18)

Although Jesus has given Christians the authority to reign in life, many are living as paupers. They have no clue what their salvation package entails. All this is down to the fact that they don't make time to consistently study their Bible. When you study your Bible regularly, you'll walk in the victory Jesus has won for you.

INTRODUCTION

I remember when I started my postgraduate research in 2014; we were given a course handbook. The handbook contained information about everything we needed to know about the course such as how to contact our supervisors, assessment deadlines and money available to students. I had a quick glance through the book only once and dashed it away. About 2 years later, I was chatting to a colleague and she was telling me some of the things that I was entitled to receive for free on the course. I was very surprised and with a confused face I asked her how she knew all this. She simply replied, "Have you read the course handbook?"

That was when I realised that I had made a big mistake, because I had missed out on many opportunities to get some free stuff. Let's be honest everyone likes freebies. For example, I had spent money on stationeries such as folders, notepads, pens and highlighters. Meanwhile, all these things were already available in the department so I didn't need to waste money on them. Furthermore, I was entitled to a specific allowance every year to help me buy books and other resources I needed for my research.

Prior to finding out about the benefits I was entitled to, I had been struggling to figure out how to get money to buy some of the academic books I needed which were quite expensive. After finally reading the course handbook, I learnt that I was supposed to apply for some stipend to purchase the books and equipment I needed. If I had initially read the course handbook, I would have avoided many of the struggles that I went through in those 2 years. I learnt a big lesson that day which was, "Read the book!"

Unfortunately, this is the story of many Christians today. They can't be bothered to read the handbook of life and so they have no idea what they're entitled to in Christ. They have no clue of the blessings that are available to them and so they are living far below God's best for their lives. When challenges knock on their door, they panic and become despondent. But it's not supposed to be so. Read the Bible to learn about the resources available in Christ so that you can overcome the challenges in life.

The Bible

The Bible is the handbook of life provided for every Christian in the journey of life. It is the most important book for every Christian. Although it was written many years ago, it has not lost its relevance. It is still as relevant today as it was then. It still possesses the same potency as when it was compiled. The principles still produce the same powerful results as ever. It can change every situation, no matter how big, when it is rightly applied.

The Bible is a mixture of law, history, poetry, biographies and autobiographies. Nonetheless, all the books relate strikingly. Written at different epochs, they all point to the Saviour of mankind, the man Jesus Christ who is fully human and fully God- 'Godman'. This is known in Christian theology as hypostatic union. It describes how Jesus Christ who is fully God, became a human being. The human nature Jesus took on, is demonstrated in the scriptures below:

> And the Word (Jesus) became flesh and dwelt among us, and we beheld His glory, the glory as of the only begotten of the Father, full of grace and truth. (John 1:14 'Jesus' added)

Elsewhere it also says,
> Without a doubt, the secret of our life of worship is great: Christ was shown to us in human form; the Spirit proved that he was right; he was seen by angels. The message about him was told to the nations; people in the world believed in him; he was taken up to heaven in glory. (1 Timothy 3:16 ERV)

The reason why Jesus came as a human being was to sacrifice His life to reconcile us to God and give us eternal life (John 3:16). Anyone who receives Jesus into his or her heart receives eternal life. Eternal life is also called Zóé life, which is the very life of God. When you have eternal life, you are now able to live a supernatural life like God. It is also important to know that only people who are saved and have eternal life will make heaven.

When Jesus was on earth, He provided the perfect example of how to live a victorious life. Jesus always knew what to say and do to overcome every challenge He faced. For example, after Jesus had fasted forty days and forty nights, He was tempted by the devil in the wilderness (Matthew 4:1-11). It should be noted that when Jesus was tempted, He didn't apply anointing oil nor did He apply fodder water. In fact, He didn't even have a praises and worship session although praises and worship is very good. Jesus simply replied with the right word. It is this right word that I call the winning word.

We need to learn to discover the winning word for every issue that comes our way. I believe that many marriages would still have been functioning today if only the couples had known the winning word to solve their problems. The barren would have been fruitful if only they knew the winning word to end barrenness. Many students would have passed their exams if only they had known the winning word. Many people would have still been alive today if only they had known the winning word to overcome death.

When we don't know the winning word, we become prey to the devil. He whispers wrong thoughts into our minds and we feel like failures, suicidal and depressed. When we don't know the winning word to overcome the devil's lies, we'll live far below God's plans for our lives. We'll accept our current position to be our destination. Locating the winning word from the scriptures in every challenge we face will ensure that we walk in continuous victory.

I want you to understand that as Christians we have been called to a life of victory, fulfillment and dominion. This book outlines some of the numerous benefits we gain from studying the Bible and how we can discover the winning word to turn every situation around. Such discoveries will enable us to enjoy life at its best, the way God intends for us.

As you go through this book, may the Holy Spirit open the eyes of your understanding and grant you the wisdom and revelation knowledge of God and His mighty power that is in His word. Amen!

CHAPTER 1
A NEW KINGDOM

The Bible is God's instructions and directions for those who have made the wisest decision, that is, the decision to put their faith in Jesus Christ the Son of God. When you put your faith in Jesus Christ as your Lord and Saviour, you are immediately and supernaturally translated from the Kingdom of Satan into the Kingdom of God.

The subject of the Kingdom of God is a big topic but I will summarise it here in order to get my point across. Simply put, the kingdom of God is the reign of Jesus Christ in our hearts. When we accept Jesus as our Lord and Saviour, we become part of His Kingdom. He comes to live in us and we also live in Him. The Bible declares that,

> "For in him we live and move and exist" (Acts 17:28). We subject ourselves to His teachings, statutes, laws and precepts. When we humble ourselves and obey His commands, we're operating in His Kingdom (1 John 3:24).

In the Kingdom of God there is joy, healing and life. So, every time Jesus heals someone or raises someone from the dead, that person has experienced a taste of the Kingdom of God. May you experience the manifestation of the Kingdom of God in Jesus name!

A New Way of living

Every child of God now dwells in the Kingdom of God. The Kingdom of God works differently from the Kingdom of Satan. For example, in the kingdom of Satan, sin is the order of the day such as lies, gossip, drunkenness and fornication (Galatians 5:19-21). On the other hand, the kingdom of God is where Jesus reigns. Righteousness, peace and joy are the way of life in this kingdom (Romans 14:17). Due to the great difference in lifestyles between the two kingdoms, the Bible (God's word) has been provided for the citizens in the Kingdom of God to embrace, learn and walk in the newness of life.

Let's look at this illustration: when a person arrives in the UK from another country, for example, from India, they quickly realise that life is very different from their home country. They must learn about life in the UK. They need to know the behaviours that are acceptable and those that are unacceptable. Furthermore, they also need to learn how to access hospitals, jobs, housing and many other things. Until they learn how to access these important things they may be stranded and may not enjoy life in the UK. Meanwhile, everything they need to enjoy life is already available. They just need to learn how to access them to enjoy them.

Similar to the illustration above, the Bible helps us to access all the goodness that God has made available to us in His Kingdom. Studying the Bible helps us to adjust our lifestyle to enjoy the best of life in God's kingdom. In addition, the Bible also shows us how to receive all the great and numerous benefits available for those who dwell permanently in the Kingdom of God.

Chapter Notes

CHAPTER 2
GOD'S MANUAL FOR VICTORIOUS LIVING

> All Scripture is given by God.
> And all Scripture is useful for teaching and for showing people what is wrong in their lives. It is useful for correcting faults and teaching the right way to live. Using the Scriptures, those who serve God will be prepared and will have everything they need to do every good work.
> (2 Timothy 3:16-17 ERV)

The Bible is our manual for maximising our lives here on earth. When you buy a new mobile phone, it comes with a manual or instructions on how to use the phone to its full capacity. However, many of us do not read the manual and so although our phones can do amazing things, we usually only know how to make phone calls, WhatsApp people and post pictures and videos on social media. We are unable to use the phone to its full potential.

One day, a colleague at university showed me an app on his black Samsung mobile phone. He explained to me how he uses the app to control the heating system in his home even from the University. He would switch on the heater, so that his house would be warm by the time he got back. I have seen and heard many other interesting things people use their smart phones to do. Many of us probably use our phones to do the mundane things. Our smart phones are heavily underused simply because we haven't sat down to explore and learn how we can use them to their full potential.

Equally, Christians who do not regularly study God's manual for life are unlikely to fulfil their potential in life. Life becomes stressful rather than successful. Everything we need for life and godliness are in the word of God and studying the word unveils our inheritance in Christ (Romans 8:17; Ephesians 1:18; 2 Peter 1:3-4). God has already prepared every resource that we need to live a prosperous and abundant life in Christ.

Today some Christians have given up in life because of their lack of knowledge of the Bible.

God's people are destroyed because of their lack of knowledge of their creator (Hosea 4:6). They have given up on their precious inheritance in this life and in the life awaiting the believer in Heaven. You need an in-depth knowledge, understanding and application of God's word to live a fulfilling Christian life.

Jesus overcame by the word

We all know that a person needs food to grow. The same is true for the Christian. We need the food of the word of God to grow from baby Christians to mature adults. For this reason, the Bible is key for the believer's growth, success and increasing faith in God. Jesus Christ was the personification of God's word (John 1:14) and defeated the devil with His superior knowledge and understanding of the word of God. Read the account of the encounter between Jesus and Satan below,

Then the Spirit led Jesus into the desert to be tempted by the devil. Jesus did not eat anything for 40 days and 40 nights. At the end of that time, he was hungry. The tempter came to him and said, "If you are the Son of God, tell these stones to become loaves of bread." Jesus answered,

"Scripture says, 'A person cannot live on bread alone but on every word that God speaks.'" Then the devil took him into the holy city and had him stand on the highest part of the temple. He said to Jesus, "If you are the Son of God, jump! Scripture says, 'He will put his angels in charge of you. They will carry you in their hands so that you never hit your foot against a rock.'" Jesus said to him, "Again, Scripture says, 'Never tempt the Lord your God.'" Once more the devil took him to a very high mountain and showed him all the kingdoms in the world and their glory. The devil said to him, "I will give you all this if you will bow down and worship me." Jesus said to him,

> "Go away, Satan! Scripture says, 'Worship the Lord your God and serve only him.'" Then the devil left him, and angels came to take care of him. (Matthew 4:1-11 GW)

In the scripture above, notice that Jesus always knew what to say to overcome each temptation. He knew the winning word to overcome the devil's advances.

We also need to know the winning word concerning the challenges and the temptations that come our way to overcome and grow in Christ.

Knowing the winning word will get you out of the most difficult situations every time. There was a time that the Scribes (teachers of the Jewish law) and the Pharisees brought a woman to Jesus who had been caught in the act of adultery. They asked Jesus whether they should stone her since this was what the Law of Moses commanded. This was a tricky situation that could have landed Jesus in big trouble. If Jesus had said, 'stone her', He would have got into trouble with the Roman law, which didn't permit the Jews to carry out their own execution. At that time, the Jews were under the rule of the Roman Empire. On the other hand, if Jesus had said they should not stone the woman, He would have contradicted the Jewish law and run into trouble with the Jewish religious leaders. Let us see what Jesus said:

> So, when they continued asking Him, He raised Himself up and said to them, "He who is without sin among you, let him throw a stone at her first." (John 8:7)

Then we see what happened after,

> Then those who heard it, being convicted by their conscience, went out one by one, beginning with the oldest even to the last. And Jesus was left alone, and the woman standing in the midst. (John 8:9)

What looked like a sticky situation was immediately diffused by the winning word. Feeding on the word gives you an edge over the enemy. If our master Jesus Christ needed God's word to overcome difficulties, then we also need it.

During his summer exams, a young man received a phone call and he was informed that his mum was gravely sick. She had developed a blood clot that blocked the flow of blood and oxygen to her brain. He knew of people who had died because of the same illness. The doctors proposed a surgery, which they admitted could lead to some life-changing side effects. Many people in the young man's position would have cried in hopelessness and understandably so. But he was very calm about the whole thing because of His faith in Jesus. He understood how powerful Jesus is and how He can turn every situation around. There is a level you get to in Christ that the problems that put other people down and makes them anxious have very little effect on your life. You just need a proper understanding of the word of God.

While he was contemplating what to do, the Holy Spirit reminded him of a scripture he knew in Revelation 1:18,

I am He who lives, and was dead, and behold, I am alive forevermore. Amen. And I have the keys of Hades and of Death.

The Holy Spirit prompted him that Jesus has the keys of death and hades. Keys here represent absolute authority. That means Jesus has complete authority over death. So, he decided to stand in the authority of Jesus and shut out death from swallowing his mum. In that instant, this scripture became so real to him that, in his imagination, he literally saw Jesus pushing the spirit of death away from his mum.
After this revelation, he became restful and at peace that the battle had been won. With this understanding, he waited on God in fasting

and prayer. In fact, while she was recovering in hospital, he was living in such peace that some of those around him didn't know he was going through such a challenge. During that period many people came to him with their prayer requests. They couldn't even tell that he was fighting a big battle. He was living in absolute peace. He knew that the battle had been won and to the glory of God this victory manifested in the natural and his mum recovered. Glory to God!

The young man located the winning word that helped him to overcome that issue. When you face any challenge, you need to find the winning word with the help of the Holy Spirit, which will guarantee your victorious outcome.

The word lifts you to the top

The winning word will also pave your way to the top places in life. We see this example in the life of Joseph. Pharaoh the King of Egypt had been informed that there is a season of 7 years of abundance coming to the land of Egypt followed by 7 years of scarcity. He needed a solution about what course of action to take. God gave Joseph the winning word to solve the problem,

Let Pharaoh do this, and let him appoint officers over the land, to collect one-fifth of the produce of the land of Egypt in the seven plentiful years. And let them gather all the food of those good years that are coming, and store up grain under the authority of Pharaoh, and let them keep food in the cities. (Genesis 41:34-35)

After Joseph had given the winning word, the King promoted him to be second in command.

Then Pharaoh said to Joseph, "Inasmuch as God has shown you all this, there is no one as discerning and wise as you. You shall be over my house, and all my people shall be ruled according to your word; only in regard to the throne will I be greater than you." And Pharaoh said to Joseph, "See, I have set you over all the land of Egypt." (Genesis 41:39-41)

The winning word changed Joseph's status from a prisoner to a prime minister overnight. The winning word will send you to places of influences.

Be Word-Filled

Unfortunately, many Christians are living far below God's expectations for their life because they are not knowledgeable about the word of God. Jesus Christ has redeemed us by His blood from the power of sin and death, for us to reign as Kings and Priests (Revelation 5:8-10), however, many Christians are living like slaves. They don't know that they have access to unlimited resources of riches, healing, peace and joy in Jesus Christ.

The lack of knowledge is mainly because many of us only open our Bibles when we're in trouble. This is not the best preparation because some problems may swallow you before you've had time to react. It is better to live ready than to get ready. Therefore, Apostle John encouraged us to seek the word of life,

> In the beginning was the Word, and the Word was with God, and the Word was God. He was in the beginning with God. All things were made through Him, and without Him nothing was made that was made. In Him was life, and the life was the light of men. And the light shines in

the darkness, and the darkness did not comprehend it. (John 1:1-5)

In other words, we need to seek the winning word before we undertake any project, get involved in any relationship, business or job. You need to discover what God is saying about it. Don't wait until the hard times come. You need to search the Bible and settle down on scriptures that the Holy Spirit teaches you. That is why John said, 'In the beginning' and not 'in the middle' or 'at the end'

As Christians, we're compared to soldiers (2 Timothy 2:3-4) and every wise army prepares for war in advance. They don't train after the battle has commenced. I read a book about the US navy and saw that they're put through intensive drills even when there is no war. They are ready for battle all year round. Thus, it is no surprise that they are widely considered to be one of the most powerful armies in the world.

By the grace of God, I've located the winning word about things that are yet to come in my life. For example, I could never see myself laying a hand on my wife, or trading punches with her.

I've come to an understanding that my role as a husband is to love my wife as Christ loves the church. Jesus loves the church unconditionally. The church is the body of Christ (you and I). Unconditional love always forgives. I've let down Jesus quite badly many times in my life but He always forgives me when I repent. So, what could my wife do to offend me so badly to turn her into a punching bag? No matter how "difficult" a woman is, love her unconditionally and she will eventually submit to you. Equally, it can generally be said that when a woman submits to a man, he'll love her. The winning word is God's manual to a life of continuous victory. It will always give you victory in every situation.

Again, I could never see my wife and I being barren. Why? Because I have seen in the word of God that one of the blessings of marriage is fruitfulness and multiplication.

> So God created man in His own image; in the image of God He created him; male and female He created them. Then God blessed them, and God said to them, "Be fruitful and multiply; fill the earth and

subdue it; have dominion over the fish of the sea, over the birds of the air, and over every living thing that moves on the earth." (Genesis 1:27-28)

Now Adam and Eve fell from glory so this was replaced by dryness and scarcity as part of the curse God placed on them. But Jesus has come to rescue me from the curse of barrenness and has positioned me in the place of the blessings and abundance (John 10:10). Because of this I cannot be barren. That issue is settled.

My point is here that we must let the word of God be the centre of our lives. When we face challenges in our lives such as disappointment, sickness, (un)employment issues, barrenness, bereavement, rejection or any other hardship, we must believe in God's word that He will work things together for our good and for His glory.

Chapter Notes

CHAPTER 3
THE BENEFITS OF GOD'S WORD

Understanding the benefits of an activity helps us to remain committed to it. For example, many young men exercise in the gym because they know that the training will help them to grow their muscles. Six benefits we gain from studying the word of God are outlined below.

Faith

Studying the word of God increases our faith. Faith should not be confused with 'hoping for the best'. Faith is also different from psychological prowess. Instead, faith is a spiritual force and the medium by which we dominate our circumstances because it makes all things possible for the believer. Faith is the avenue that we receive from heaven whether it is money, healing or prosperity.

One day a father brought his son who had an evil spirit to Jesus. Wherever the spirit took hold of the boy, he would shake violently and foam at the mouth, and then become stiff. Jesus said to the despaired father,

> "As far as possibilities go, everything is possible for the person who believes." (Mark 9:23)

Faith is not positive thinking. Positive thinking cannot cast out an evil spirit. But the force of faith can! Faith works by connecting the believer to God, who then intervenes in his/her situation. Faith puts us in a position to receive from God and when God takes over your situation, it is over! The author of Hebrews stated that if we don't receive the word of God with faith, the message wouldn't benefit us (Hebrews 4:2). This is because without faith it is impossible to please God (Hebrews 11:6).

It must also be noted that there are different measures of faith. When you are saved, God gives you some measure of faith, however, it is your responsibility to develop your faith.

> For by the grace given to me, I tell everyone among you not to think of himself more

highly than he should think. Instead, think sensibly, as God has distributed a measure of faith to each one. (Romans 12:3 HCSB)

There are at least 5 types of faith referred to in the Bible. They are:

Common faith - To Titus, a true son in our common faith: Grace, mercy, and peace from God the Father and the Lord Jesus Christ our Savior. (Titus 1:4 HCSB)

All believers who have accepted Jesus as their Lord and Saviour share this faith. Common faith is also known as saving faith.

No Faith - But He said to them, "Why are you so fearful? How is it that you have no faith?" (Mark 4:40)

Jesus asked his disciples this question during a stormy trip on the sea. The disciples were panicking because of the storms that beat against the boat. Now the question is: where was their faith? It was finished! If we don't build our faith, we may face some violent trials that will push us to breaking point and eventually drown us.

Little Faith - Immediately Jesus reached out His hand, caught hold of him, and said to him,

> "You of little faith, why did you doubt?" (Matthew 14:31 HCSB)

Little faith can only believe God for little things. Little faith is understandable for a new Christian but God wants you to build your faith. Little faith can only deliver little results.

Great Faith - Then Jesus said to her,

> "Woman, you have great faith! Your request is granted." And her daughter was healed at that moment. (Matthew 15:28 NIV)

Jesus described the woman's faith as great because of her persistence. She persisted until she secured the attention of Jesus to heal her daughter who was demon possessed. Great faith doesn't give up. It persists until God answers.

The Gift of Faith - The same Spirit gives faith to one person... (1st Corinthians 12:9). The gift of faith is different from little faith and great faith. The gift of faith is one of the nine gifts of the Holy Spirit (1 Corinthians 12:1-11). This type of faith is a supernatural ability the Holy Spirit gives us to believe God for unusual results. The gift of faith is not something you can work for but a supernatural endowment the Holy Spirit imparts into us.

The way to build your faith is through a diligent study of God's word.

So then faith comes by hearing, and hearing by the word of God. (Romans 10:17)

When you apply God's word with faith, you'll always get results. One day a young man in his final year at university was required to complete a dissertation as part of his course. A dissertation is a major research project final years are usually required to undertake especially those in the field of Social science (Social Policy, Sociology and Psychology). Every student is allocated a supervisor who guides the student to complete the research project. This young man was paired with a supervisor who was reputed to be a very strict marker. This can be a disadvantage as the supervisor marks the dissertation project in most cases and ideally you want a generous marker.

He became concerned when he discovered who his supervisor was. The dissertation carries a significant percentage of your overall university grades so you can imagine how important it is. Immediately, he went to search the scriptures to locate the winning word to turn the situation into his favour. He read Psalms 5:12 which said, For You, O Lord, will bless the righteous; With favour You will surround him as with a shield.

A righteous person is one whose sins have been forgiven and cleansed by the blood of Jesus. As a result, they have been made right with God. He saw from that passage that as a person redeemed by the blood of Jesus, he was blessed and highly favoured by God. Consequently, he'll find favour with the supervisor. He prayed based on this word and God answered. The supervisor turned out to be extremely supportive. For example, there was a time when the supervisor wasn't responding to emails from other students but he always responded promptly to the young man's emails. In the end, he was awarded a distinction in his project and his grade was in the top 5 on the course. Glory to God! His faith in God's word turned things around. There's no issue that is difficult for God.

This formula works:
Winning word + faith + prayer + action=
accomplishment

He located the winning word (Psalms 5:12), his faith rose and with prayers and hardwork overcame. You'll always get results when you seek the winning word and apply it by faith.

Understanding the will of God

God's word helps us to understand the will of God and how He functions. This is crucial because for any relationship to be successful, the parties involved ought to understand each other's character.

> Two people will not walk together unless they have agreed to do so. (Amos 3:3 ERV)

We ought to know God's will for us to be able to align our will with His. What is God's will? It is revealed in His word. For example, God's will is for everyone to be saved,

> ...who(God) wants all people to be saved and to come to a knowledge of the truth. (1 Timothy 2:4 NIV 'God' added).

Knowing and doing God's will was one of the main reasons why Jesus had an eternal impact on earth in just three and half years of ministry. Jesus stated that,

> For I have come down from heaven, not to do My own will, but the will of Him who sent Me. (John 6:38)

Doing the will of God produces results in our prayer lives. The author of Hebrews said,

> You need to persevere so that when you have done the will of God, you will receive what he has promised. (Hebrews 10:36 NIV)

Pray the will of God in your life and begin to see things fall into place for you.

Enter into God's Rest

Knowing God's word and praying His will for your life ushers you into the rest of God. Entering God's rest is the point when God takes over your battles because you have understood His majesty and have surrendered your life to Him. The author of Hebrews thus encouraged us to enter God's rest,

For anyone who enters God's rest also rests from their works, just as God did from his. Let us, therefore, make every effort to enter that rest, so that no one will perish by following their example of disobedience. (Hebrews 4:10-11 NIV) Rest speaks of the believer's eternal home with Christ in heaven. However, it also includes our current spiritual residence in Christ where we dwell in the presence of Jesus and the joy we experience in his presence (Ephesians 2:4-6). We become strong when we're filled with joy because the joy of the Lord is our strength (Nehemiah 8:10). When we enter rest, worrying and anxiety stop. We remain joyful and strong during challenges. There is no room for depression for a believer who has entered God's rest. Jesus demonstrated the perfect example of how life is for a Christian who has understood the will of God and entered rest. If you're still having sleepless nights over your education, marriage, job, ministry or any other issue, it means you haven't entered rest concerning it. You must keep praying and believing God until your heart is at peace.

Inheritance

God's word also helps us to understand our new status and inheritance in Christ Jesus. As we share in His sufferings, we'll also share in His glory. Our inheritance includes but are not limited to the following:

Spiritual Blessings

> Blessed be the God and Father of our Lord Jesus Christ, who has blessed us with every spiritual blessing in the heavenly places in Christ. (Ephesians 1:3)

Spiritual blessings include forgiveness of sins, redemption through the blood of Jesus and our new status as children of God.

Eternal life

> For God so loved the world that He gave His only begotten Son, that whoever believes in Him should not perish but have everlasting life. (John 3:16)

The Holy Spirit imparts eternal life (also called everlasting life) into a person who accepts Jesus as their Lord and Saviour. Eternal life is

God depositing His life into us, so that we can live like Him. When you have eternal life, you have God's life.

As people who have God's nature, we should no longer live in sin. When we are saved, our old sinful nature that we inherited from Adam is removed, and we receive a new, godly nature that craves the things of God (2 Corinthians 5:17). When we have God's nature, we love what God loves and hate what He hates. What does God love and hate? All is revealed in His word. For example, we can see that God loves righteousness but hates sin (Hebrews 1:9). When you have eternal life, physical death is merely a passage into God's presence.

Jesus Christ is the embodiment of God's nature. He provided the perfect model of how a person who has received God's nature should live. Jesus was full of the Holy Spirit and He walked in holiness and purity. We can also see that Jesus was obedient to God (Philippians 2:5-8); did not sin (2 Corinthians 5:21); loved people (John 15:12-13) and always did good works (Acts 10:38).

We are now able to resist any sinful habit that we had before we got saved. When we pray, the Holy Spirit will give us the power that we need to overcome. If we pray but continue to struggle in sin, then we ought to engage in fasting (Mark 9:29). It is also a good idea to confide in a matured Christian to counsel and support you. I have found this to be very helpful in my life.

I remember there was a time in my teenage years that I used to struggle with sexual sins. I prayed about it and seemed to be doing well only to fall back into it. I was always in church and did everything possible to overcome this struggle. I found it very difficult to talk to anyone about it because it was rarely treated and also, I didn't want to look like the "worst sinner". It was not until I spoke to one of my leaders to receive support that I managed to break free. The church needs to discuss these topics regularly rather than just preaching about it, so that people will find it easier to come forward and receive support.

A new spiritual position with Christ in the heavenly places

> Yes, it is because we are a part of Christ Jesus that God raised us from death and seated us together with him in the heavenly places. God did this so that his kindness to us who belong to Christ Jesus would clearly show for all time to come the amazing richness of his grace. (Ephesians 2:6-7 ERV)

Another inheritance we have in Jesus Christ is a new spiritual position. Every believer is supernaturally given a new position in heaven. The Bible states that we are seated together with Jesus at the right hand of God (Mark 16:19; Ephesians 2:6-7). The right hand of God is a place of honour, authority and power. We are seated together with Jesus in the very presence of God! Hallelujah! Moreover, we also dwell in Christ (1 John 4:12-13). This is a mystery: we live on earth, dwell in Christ and are seated with Jesus in heavenly places (Ephesians 2:5-6).

For the believer, this means that heaven is our source and the earth is our resource.

Take for instance when you buy bread from a supermarket such as Tesco or Sainsbury's, that is the resource. The actual source of that bread is the bakery shop where it was baked. God can give us money through our jobs (resource) but God is our provider (source).

For this reason, believers we don't rely on the system of the world but the system of God. We need to come to a place where we have a 'God is my source' mentality. This thinking has enabled me to tap into heaven's provision at will.

One day I needed money to pay for my tuition fees. The money took so long to be paid that the University suspended my student login details. I couldn't access my lecture slides, reading list and other important information.

While studying the Bible, a scripture that I have known for many years came alive in my spirit. It suddenly hit me that God has unlimited riches in heaven. The scripture says,

> And my God shall supply all your need according to His riches in glory by Christ Jesus. (Philippians 4:19)

I told God in prayer that He needs to send me the money because He as unlimited money in heaven. Then one day God spoke to me to bless a particular individual and I obeyed promptly, with the little money I had. A couple of weeks later, a relative also came to bless me with the money to pay for my tuition fees.

Having a 'God is my source' mentality puts you in control of the challenges that come your way. As citizens of heaven, we are not limited to the resources in this world. We have a great inheritance in Christ Jesus. Learn to rely on God. It is your avenue to great achievements

God's word opens the door to a life of great achievements. The great characters in the Bible studied and applied the scriptures in their lives. Although they have gone to be with the Lord, their works are still speaking today. Biblical figures such as Abraham, Moses, David, Hannah, Elizabeth (the mother of John the Baptist) to name a few are still talked about today. More recent giants such as Smith Wigglesworth, Kathryn Kuhlman, Kenneth Hagin and T.L. Osborn were all people of great exploits. They were industrious students of the Word of God and became Kingdom giants. We can also become men and women of exploits when we get addicted to the ever reliable and unchanging word of God. God commanded Joshua in this way,

> Always remember what is written in that book of law. Speak about that book and study it day and night. Then you can be sure to obey what is written there. If you do this, you will be wise and successful in everything you do. (Joshua 1:8 ERV)

Notice that God didn't 'advise' Joshua to be obedient. Obeying God's word is not an option nor a choice but a command. Obeying God's word empowers us to live a life of great exploits. Your life becomes a living testimony and a reference point for others.

Manifestation of God's power

God's word releases God's power. It is vital for you to know that the extent of the manifestation of God's power in our lives depends on the measure of His word in us. The more of God's word that is in us, the stronger our faith becomes and we experience His manifestation in our lives. We see in the story of creation in Genesis chapter 1, a manifestation of God's word releasing God's power. In Genesis 1 verse 3, God said, "let there be light and there was light." Following that we see a pattern of "God said…it was." When God's word is spoken, the desired change is created. In other words when we speak God's word, whatever we declare is created.

The man Job knew the power that is loaded in God's word. He stated,

> You will also declare a thing, and it will be established for you; So light will shine on your ways. (Job 22:28)

Get into God's word and make declarations to release God's power into your life to change any situation.
This is because God watches over his word to perform it (Jeremiah 1:12). If you want God to perform great things in your life, then have a great measure of His word in you.

The benefits of God's word for the believer is not limited to those outlined in this chapter. There are many more that you can probably think of that have not been mentioned.

Chapter Notes

CHAPTER 4
THE SURE FOUNDATION

My private Bible study or 'Quiet time' as some call it, is the sure foundation that my life is built on, in addition to daily fellowship with the Holy Spirit. Any wise builder builds a house on a solid foundation. Jesus told a story about the wise man who built his life on the rock of God's word and the foolish builder who built on sand (sand can mean relying on anything else apart from Jesus such as jobs, money, self-confidence). Jesus said,

> Therefore whoever hears these sayings of Mine, and does them, I will liken him to a wise man who built his house on the rock: and the rain descended, the floods came, and the winds blew and beat on that house; and it did not fall, for it was founded on the rock. "But everyone who hears these sayings of Mine, and does not do them, will be like a foolish man who built his house on the sand: and the rain descended, the floods came, and the winds blew and beat on that house; and it fell. And great was its fall." (Matthew 7:24-27)

The Bible is a rock-solid foundation. When you build on a solid foundation you can survive earthquakes, strong floods and hurricanes, which represent the fiery trials and tests of life. You become strong and immovable. For example, the floods of life that trouble others cannot overcome me because my foundation is built on the word of God. The word of God has enabled me to survive very difficult circumstances that even killed others. The word of God can be trusted because it is robust, durable and dependable. That is why the Bible says,

Heaven and earth will pass away, but My words will by no means pass away. (Matthew 24:35)
This scripture shows that only the Bible can stand the test of time. The word of God created the universe and has sustained it since creation and will continue to sustain the universe until Jesus comes. The Bible says,

> God, who at various times and in various ways spoke in time past to the fathers by the prophets, has in these last days spoken to us by His Son, whom He has appointed heir of all things, through whom

also He made the worlds; who being the brightness of His glory and the express image of His person, and upholding all things by the word of His power, when He had by Himself purged our sins, sat down at the right hand of the Majesty on high, (Hebrews 1:1-3)

If God's word has sustained the entire universe since inception, it has more than enough capacity to sustain your life. This makes the word of God a trustworthy and reliable foundation to build your life on.

It is dangerous to build on any other foundation such as money, jobs and health. These things are very good but they don't last. Money can fail (Genesis 47:15), you can lose your job, and your health can deteriorate but only God's word abides forever. It is wisdom to build on the strong and rock solid foundation- that is the word of God. Nothing in life can defeat God's word, not even death. When Lazarus died in John chapter 11, we see that Jesus (who is the word of God) called Lazarus back to life.

The word of God has brought me to where I am today and it is taking me to my destination. It has rescued me from difficult places and has made me wiser. Most of my understanding of the Bible comes from my private Bible study session. A lot of the things I share in this book is borne out of hours of Bible study over the years. It is possible to spend hours in a single Bible study session. We need to make studying God's word a priority. It is dangerous to spend 3 hours or more on social media and other activities but not be able to spend even 30 minutes studying the Bible. You need to be loaded with God's word to overcome the stormy days ahead.

Maybe you might be thinking that you haven't really studied and relied on the Bible up until now but your life is okay. God is admonishing you through this book to change your ways so that you can be better prepared for the journey ahead. To fail to prepare, is to prepare to fail. God overlooked our ignorance in the past because we didn't know any better but He is calling us to get into His word.

God overlooked the times when people didn't know any better. But now he commands everyone everywhere to turn to him and change the way they think and act. (Acts 17:30 GW)

Bible Study Guidelines

We need to come to a place where we enjoy studying the Bible. When you enjoy doing an activity, it becomes a part of you. Below are some guidelines on how to have an effective Bible study. These are not rigid procedures but some general principles to help us to have an effective personal Bible study.

An easy to understand Bible

There are many Christians who read their Bible almost exclusively during church service. I believe that one of the main reasons for this is that they own Bible translations that are difficult to understand. Consequently, reading the Bible becomes a boring experience. However, having an-easy-to-understand Bible is important because it is easier to process the information and thus making your Bible study experience more enjoyable.

Modern technology such as Bible apps has made it easier to have numerous Bible translations at our fingertips. We can read the Bible on our daily commutes to school, universities or work. Take advantage of these apps.

Notebook

At school, we use exercise books to jot down information about the things we learn. In the same way, every serious Bible student needs a specially assigned notebook to record his or her findings from studying the Bible. Notebooks are important because written records help us to remember the important lessons and the wisdom we receive from God's word. In Revelation 12:11, the word of God is part of the weapons that defeated the devil along with the precious blood of Jesus.

> And they overcame him by the blood of the Lamb and by the word of their testimony, and they did not love their lives to the death. (Revelation 12:11)

Testimony involves evidence or records. They may be in oral (by mouth) or written form. Having written notes (words) helps us to overcome the devil. Jesus used written records of the word of God to overcome the devil- "It is written..." (Matthew 4:1-11). Without writing what you have learnt from your Sunday services and private Bible study sessions, you're very likely to forget the valuable insights and lessons you have gained.

In the parable of the sower (Matthew 13:1-23), Jesus speaks about a second group of people who receive the word of God with joy but give up as soon as they have problems or persecution. I believe that this second group of hearers are people who do not write notes to remind them of the insights they have gained from God's word. For this reason, they give up in times of trouble. You need to keep written records too.

Prayer

Prayer and the Word of God work together. It is like eating food (the Word of God) and drinking water (Prayer). When you eat and don't drink enough water, you're likely to get constipated. Similarly, when you drink lots of water and do not eat enough food, you are unlikely to function at your maximum level.

Apostle Paul prayed for the church in Ephesus to receive spiritual insight and revelation of our Lord Jesus Christ. He prayed that,

> ...the God of our Lord Jesus Christ, the Father of glory, may give to you the spirit of wisdom and revelation in the knowledge of Him, the eyes of your understanding being enlightened; that you may know what is the hope of His calling, what are the riches of the glory of His inheritance in the saints, and what is the exceeding greatness of His power toward us who believe, according to the working of His mighty power which He worked in Christ when He raised Him from the dead and seated Him at His right hand in the heavenly places, far above all principality and power and might and dominion, and every name that is named, not only in this age but also in that which is to come. (Ephesians 1:17-21)

The late American preacher Kenneth Hagin said that he regularly meditated on and prayed using the scripture above. Just like Apostle Paul, Kenneth Hagin sought the revelation and insights of the word of God from the Holy

Spirit. He was a man of great biblical insight according to the measure the Holy Spirit gave him. So prayer is important to gain deep spiritual understanding of the Bible and consequently have an effective Bible study.

Sometimes there are hindrances that stop God from answering our prayers. Sin is the main barrier to answered prayers. Sin literally means missing the mark. It is essentially doing something that is contradictory to the word of God. The Bible is full of examples of sin (Genesis 3; Proverbs 6:16-19; Galatians 5:19-21). We need to be very mindful of what I term emotional sins: unforgiveness, bitterness, hatred and anger. Although anger is not a sin, it can easily lead to sin.

> "In your anger do not sin": Do not let the sun go down while you are still angry, and do not give the devil a foothold. (Ephesians 4:26-27 NIV)

I believe emotional sins are dangerous because they give the devil a legitimate opportunity to cause havoc in our lives. Emotional sins can creep into our hearts and we tend to justify them.

For example, everyone (including unbelievers) knows that stealing is wrong. However, when it comes to emotional sins, sometimes we don't forgive those who offend us and get bitter about them, which can lead to hatred or strong dislike towards them. Even worse, we justify our ill feelings and pretend it is okay. I have heard many testimonies about people received their physical healing after they agreed to forgive those who hurt them. If you have any bitterness or unforgiveness towards someone, approach them about it and pray for the Holy Spirit to help you to let it go. Having a clean heart and a pure conscience is needed to have greater access and understanding of the word of God.

Holy Spirit

Have you ever been to a service or listened to a sermon that the preacher made the Bible so interesting, relevant and practical that you were inspired to read your Bible? Yes, I have too! Some of my favourite preachers have so much understanding and insight of the Bible that I used to wonder if they used a special translation of the Bible made just for them. It was later on that I realised it was the Holy Spirit that teaches them the Bible.

We need to engage with the Holy Spirit for a profitable Bible study. The Greek word for the Holy Spirit is parakletos meaning comforter, advocate and helper. Indeed, the Holy Spirit helps us to understand God's word and gives us revelation knowledge of God (John 14:26). Revelation knowledge simply means the Holy Spirit uncovering some hidden truths beyond the words we read in the scriptures.

When I was doing my dissertation/thesis, I collected data using interviews and during the data analysis, my supervisor said to me, "Michael, look beyond the data." I didn't really understand what he meant and it took me a week to figure it out. He was basically saying dig deeper into what the interviewees told you. Don't just write out their responses. Go beyond the words to understand what they're really thinking. This is similar to divine revelation. The Holy Spirit uncovers biblical truths beyond the pages of the scriptures we read. Revelation knowledge allows us to gain a deeper knowledge and understanding of God's word.

Apostle Paul was a man who had great spiritual insight. In 1 Corinthians 15:53-55, the Holy Spirit gave him a revelation about the rapture and the second coming of Christ. The Holy Spirit is instrumental in teaching us and revealing God's mind to us. The Holy Spirit is the master teacher of the word of God. We see from the verse below:

> But you have received the Holy Spirit, and he lives within you, so you don't need anyone to teach you what is true. For the Spirit teaches you everything you need to know, and what he teaches is true-it is not a lie. So just as he has taught you, remain in fellowship with Christ. (1 John 2:27 NLT)

What this also means for us is that when we are taught a biblical doctrine, we have the anointing from the Holy Spirit which explains God's word to us. Every doctrine we hear must be compared to the scriptures to test if they agree, just as the people of Berea practised (Acts 17:11).

In addition to giving us revelation knowledge of the word of God, the Holy Spirit works in us and changes our hearts to produce fruits (Galatians 5:22-23). These fruits represent our moral character and the Holy Spirit helps us to think and act more like Jesus. The Holy Spirit helps us to become an example of Christ. This is what God expects of us.

Understanding

Understanding is very crucial to a successful Bible study. In the parable of the sower, the seed that fell on good ground produced fruits of 30, 60 and 100 fold (Matthew 13:23). The differences reflected the level of understanding of the hearers. Thus, the extent of your fruitfulness depends on your level of understanding. That is why Proverbs 4:7 says, "... so use everything you have to get understanding."

To really get a deeper understanding of the Bible and correctly interpret scripture, you must consider the following points and how they influence what has been written: the biblical context (what has been said before that verse and after), the historical context, the cultural context, geographic context and the total biblical context (allowing scripture to interpret scripture). When you consider the points mentioned during your study time, you open yourself up to gaining deeper understanding of the Bible.

It is also a good idea to research on Bible passages you don't understand. It may mean spending a significant amount of time on just a verse or phrase. Understanding is key to a fruitful Bible study. Do not read something for the sake of it. Seek understanding!

Consistency

Consistency is key to a fruitful Bible study. Gym enthusiasts will tell you that it is better to spend half an hour in the gym each day from Monday to Friday, than to spend 3 hours in just one day of the week. Similarly, in relation to food, it is more beneficial for the body to eat daily than weekly. As you feed on God's word daily, you grow stronger and wiser each day.

Meditation

Meditation involves thinking, pondering or reflecting on God's word. God told Joshua to meditate on the Law day and night so that he will be prosperous (Joshua 1:8). Meditating over God's word makes us God-conscious and as a result, we are more likely to walk in holiness and purity. I believe that it was the meditation on God's word that enabled Joseph to escape the advances of Potiphar's wife. A God-conscious

Joseph said that he couldn't sin against God (Genesis 39:9). Meditating on God's word helps us to carefully apply it in our daily walk and thus helps us to overcome temptation. Through meditation, the Holy Spirit also sheds more light on God's word in our hearts. In other words, He gives us deeper understanding of God's word.

I was invited to minister at a programme at Hull University, located in the North-eastern part of England and about 322 kilometres from London. The theme of the programme was 'Waymaker' taken from Isaiah 43:19,

> Behold, I will do a new thing, Now it shall spring forth; Shall you not know it? I will even make a road in the wilderness and rivers in the desert.

> I read the entire chapter but decided to meditate on this verse in order to understand what God wanted me to know concerning that statement. Then the Holy Spirit showed me that Jesus is the Waymaker. Jesus made this explicitly known in John 14:6,

Jesus said to him, "I am the way, the truth, and the life. No one comes to the Father except through Me.

God was saying that there was a coming Saviour who was Jesus. He will make the way out of our wilderness of sin, sickness, sorrow, death and many other things the devil has plagued us with. The rivers in Isaiah 43:19 represented the Holy Spirit (John 7:37-39). So Jesus rescues us from our wilderness of sin and the Holy Spirit empowers us to continue living in this freedom. Such understanding is not obvious just by reading the scripture in Isaiah but through meditation, the Holy Spirit opens our understanding.

Declaration

The power in the word comes alive when it is declared; that is spoken out aloud or professed even when others doubt us. You need to declare God's word to have the desired outcome. It is not enough to meditate on the Word; you need to declare the Word. God told Ezekiel to speak His word to bring life and restoration to a spiritually dead people.

Also He said to me, "Prophesy to the breath, prophesy, son of man, and say to the breath, 'Thus says the Lord God: "Come from the four winds, O breath, and breathe on these slain, that they may live."'" 10 So I prophesied as He commanded me, and breath came into them, and they lived, and stood upon their feet, an exceedingly great army. (Ezekiel 37:9-10 HCSB) You may ask, "but what if I am declaring but I'm not seeing any results?" You continue to speak until you see the desired change in the situation. Elijah declared the word continually until he got his breakthrough at the seventh time (1Kings 18:41-19:8). Remember this:

> What you don't say, you won't see.
> What you don't profess, you won't possess.

I have trained myself over the years to speak only positive things into my life even during challenging times. For example, I don't profess that I have a headache. Instead, I say, "I am recovering from a headache." Even when we are physically weak, in Christ we are strong (2 Corinthians 12:10). I believe it is better to say, "I'm healed in Jesus name" than to keep professing sickness. I'm not saying that you should deny the fact that you are sick but it is better to profess healing than sickness.

> We need to discipline ourselves to profess God's word in every situation we face. When the word of God becomes more real to us than our challenges, we'll get more results and begin to see the greater works Jesus spoke about (John 14:12).

Sometimes my friends mock me and say that I am over spiritual and not realistic. Reality depends on your perception. For example, Moses sent 12 spies to Canaan to check out the land and bring back a report (Numbers 13). Today, the land of Canaan includes Lebanon, Israel, Palestine, North-western Jordan, and some Western areas of Syria. They returned from spying the land after 40 days. Out of the 12 spies, 10 of them said they saw powerful giants but 2 of them, Joshua and Caleb, saw powerless giants. They all saw the same adversaries but had different perception. Joshua and Caleb saw them and thought although these giants are tall, our God is the most high. On the other hand, the 10 spies saw the giants and became afraid of their size. We need to discipline ourselves to see things through the eyes of faith. Our God is greater than every giant (challenges) we face in our lives.

Avoid distractions

When you are involved in a deep communication with an important person such as your spouse, children, siblings, job recruitment agents, you try your best to avoid any distraction. You are unlikely to fiddle with your mobile phone or allow anything to distract you.

This principle applies to your Bible study time. It is wise to avoid all forms of distractions even if that means putting away your mobile phone, switching off your TV and getting off social media. When you are focused on God through His word, you are more likely to hear when He speaks. It is difficult to hold a meaningful conversation when you are distracted. That is why we need to avoid all forms of distractions.

Music

One of the biggest distractions for Christians today is our choice of music. I remember during my university days, a relatively well-known preacher came to talk about relationships, particularly dating between young men and women. He mentioned that he used to be depressed all the time but didn't know the reason. One day, God told him to stop listening to a particular music because that was causing his depression. Surprisingly, the song was only the instrumentals. When he obeyed God and stopped listening to the song, the depression ceased.

Prior to hearing this testimony, the Holy Spirit had convicted me several times that if I want to get deeper into the things of God, I need to listen to gospel songs and stop listening to secular songs. I found this very difficult to obey. I had over 1000 songs and I was a big fan of Lil Wayne. I knew the lyrics to almost all his songs. His music was mostly about sex, money and drugs.

Even though the Holy Spirit convicted me, I used to justify my actions and engaged in several debates that it was okay to listen to secular songs. It wasn't easy but I eventually thought to myself that I've made many sacrifices to live for God so if this is the last hurdle to get deeper then I'm ready to let go. I deleted all my secular songs and got a gospel playlist. Let me be honest here, it made a massive difference to my walk with God. One of the biggest impacts it has had on my life is that it made it so much easier to hear God's voice and recognise the promptings of the Holy Spirit.

Several years later, one of my friends posted on Facebook that when he stopped listening to secular songs, he could clearly hear God's voice. This shows that it wasn't a unique experience for me but something that'll happen for every believer. I believe that one of the reasons why it becomes easier to hear from God is because gospel music silences the voice of others and amplifies the voice of God. There are at least 4 voices that speak to us namely: our mind, the voice of others, the voice of Satan and the voice of God. The voice we pay the most attention to, will amplify in our minds and eventually reflect in our lives. If for example, we listen to violent Rap songs, R&B and Afro beats then the voice of those artistes will amplify in our minds and lives. But if we listen to gospel songs, then the voice of the Holy Spirit will amplify in our minds and lives.

The question is which voice are you listening to the most? Which voice is amplified in your life? In 2007, I bumped into one of my friends that I went to school with, on my way to the barbershop. During our brief catch up, he started telling me about this rap song he'd been listening to. At that time, there was a rapper on the scene whose lyrics were mainly about stabbing people, taking drugs in the club and sex. In his own words, my friend said, " I swear if I listen to this guy all day, I'll probably get a knife and stab someone. He's too sick though." My thoughts were, "but it's only a song why would you do that?" But I fully understand it now. The rapper's voice was what he was listening to the most and it was amplifying in his mind. Someone might say, "Well, I listen to those songs and don't feel like stabbing someone or doing drugs or having sex." That may be the case for now but it surely is having a negative effect on you in one-way or another.

It is just like the preacher who came to my university who was being affected by a secular song but didn't even know it. So your choice of music determines which voice will amplify in your mind. Listen to gospel songs that will amplify the voice of God in your mind so that you can hear clearly from Heaven.

Another issue about music choice is not only about the voice we hear but also the kind of spirits we invite into our lives. What we need to understand is that music attracts spirits. One day the Kings of Judah, Israel and Edom were going to war and went to enquire from a Prophet called Elisha whether they'll be victorious in the battle. To create the right atmosphere to clearly hear from God, Prophet Elisha asked for a harp to be played.

But now bring me a musician.
> **"Then it happened, when the musician played, that the hand of the Lord came upon him. (2 Kings 3:15)**

We see that God's hand, which can also mean God's power, Spirit or presence, came on Elisha and he began to hear from God. The interesting thing about this story is that there were no lyrics. The instrumentals alone were enough to draw God's Spirit. Therefore, the music you choose to listen to will determine what spirits you're inviting into your life. The kind of spirit the song brings depends on whether that artiste is saved, meaning that, the singer has accepted Jesus as his/her Lord and Saviour. If that is the case then it'll surely reflect in their lives and music. The Bible makes it clear that by their fruits you shall know them.

> You will know these people because of what they do. Good things don't come from people who are bad, just as grapes don't come from thornbushes, and figs don't come from thorny weeds. (Matthew 7:16 ERV)

A saved singer will produce Holy Spirit filled songs. Spirit filled songs are not necessarily slow worship style songs but any songs which draw you closer to Jesus.

> Let the teaching of Christ live inside you richly. Use all wisdom to teach and counsel each other. Sing psalms, hymns, and spiritual songs with thankfulness in your hearts to God. Everything you say and everything you do should be done for Jesus your Lord. And in all you do, give thanks to God the Father through Jesus.
> (Colossians 3:16-17 ERV)

Thank God we have many born again musicians such as Sinach, Travis Greene, Donnie McClurkin, Don Moen and many others. Let us make the most of these artistes. We need to avoid songs that take our minds away from Jesus and into promiscuous thoughts, violence and many ungodly desires. Most of the secular songs now are mainly about sex, drugs and money. They're piercing our souls and weakening our desire to pray, study the Bible, and live for God.

I also recognise that there are songs that are not necessarily gospel but sends out a positive message about love and unity or some other positive cause. It's up to you to decide whether you listen to these songs or otherwise. My main point is that if we desire to hear from God and be able to recognise the leading of the Holy Spirit, then let us engage in songs that draw us to Jesus. Spiritual songs will spur us to pray. They will also exhort and edify us.

These guidelines outlined above will help the God-hungry believer to have an encounter with God and His word in their Bible study and thus make the Bible study an enjoyable experience.

Chapter notes

CHAPTER 5
THE BIBLE STUDY SESSION

Let us look at some commonly asked questions about the Bible study session.

What is the best time of the day?

Although you can have your Bible studies at anytime during the day, the mornings are probably the best time because it gives you an opportunity to start the day with God's word. This was the practice of Jesus.

> The next morning Jesus woke up very early. He left the house while it was still dark and went to a place where he could be alone and pray. (Mark 1:35 ERV)

However, you can choose the most suitable time in the day.

What should I read?

You can choose to read a chapter in the Bible or do a systematic study of a book, for example, John. Some people also read a devotional guide such as Daily Bread in addition to the Bible. In my church, we have the 'book of the month' (BOTM), where the Pastor selects a book from the Bible for everyone to study. I find it very encouraging to study and discuss the lessons we are learning from the BOTM with my fellow church members during our home cell fellowship.

How do I study the Bible?

After reading a passage or chapter from the Bible, you should reflect by asking the following questions:

> What is God teaching me?
> Have I learnt something about God, Jesus and the Holy Spirit?
> Are there mistakes I need to correct in my life?
> Are there sins I need to avoid?
> Is there a character or virtue I need to improve?
> Is there a blessing for me to enjoy?
> Record the answers in a notebook as God speaks to your heart.

Prayer

It is always very important to pray before you study the Bible and ask the Holy Spirit to give you a deeper understanding of what you are reading. Personally, I have found it useful to pray using Ephesians 1:15 to 23. At the end of your Bible study, it is beneficial to pray about the lessons you have learnt and ask the Holy Spirit to help you implement them in your life.
Meditation

As you go about your day's business, you should meditate on the lessons from your Bible study sessions and the Holy Spirit will give you more understanding.

Locating the winning word

In chapter 4, I touched on the the parable of the wise and the foolish builder (Matthew 7:24-27). One thing that is certain in life is that everyone will go through some stormy times. However, the strength of your foundation will determine if your experience will be stressful or restful during those difficult times.

When the challenges of life show up, we can search the Bible to find scriptures that addresses that situation. An easy route is to use Google or other search engines. For example, we can search for "Bible verse in difficult times" or "finding peace in Jesus".

Many Christians use this route and I do occasionally but the only problem is that sometimes you may not have Internet access. Another option is to use the subject index at the back of your Bible. Although not all Bibles may have this useful information, most study Bibles have it.

The main issue with both methods is that problems don't always give you advance warning before they come. There are some challenges that may crush your spirit before you've had a chance to react. An example is the young man's testimony about his mum who was suddenly attacked by the spirit of death. The panic may unsettle you.

The best preparation is studying, memorising and meditating on God's word at all times and soaking it into your spirit man. When you're challenged, the Holy Spirit will remind you of a word you already know.

You remind people of something they already have an idea about. Jesus said concerning the Holy Spirit,

> But the Helper, the Holy Spirit, whom the Father will send in My name, He will teach you all things, and bring to your remembrance all things that I said to you. (John 14:26)

From my experience, it is rare for God to give you a word you have never read about or even heard before.

There was a time that I was struggling in my Master's degree at King's College London. I was working so hard but my results were not reflecting my hard work. I found the first part of the semester very difficult because there were a lot of new concepts I had to learn which I had no previous knowledge of. Nonetheless, I was very determined to do well. If you want to go far in life you need to have grit and determination beyond measure. I felt like giving up many times and there were times where I was close to tears fearing that I was going to fail.

At the beginning of the second semester, the Holy Spirit prompted me of a scripture I had heard before, that I have the mind of Christ.

> For "who has known the mind of the Lord that he may instruct Him?" But we have the mind of Christ.
> (1 Corinthians 2:16)

I asked myself this question, "If Jesus was taking my course would He have been failing?" No! I realised that Jesus would have got distinctions. If I have the mind of Jesus then I should be getting distinctions. That insight turned things around drastically. It gave me a new perspective to go on and do better. I waited on God using that scripture and my results changed from that point on. I went from getting pass grades to getting distinctions. In the end, I finished with a merit overall. Glory to God! When you stay consistently in God's word, the Holy Spirit will bring you the winning word. The winning word will bring victory out of every situation.

Chapter Notes

Chapter Notes

CHAPTER 6
OBEY THE WORD

Sat-navs (satellite navigation) have become part of our lifestyle today. Sat-navs provide useful information when you're travelling such as the fastest routes, possible delays, duration of the journey and much more. But the comfort of your journey and whether you'll arrive at your destination depends on how accurately you follow the instructions on the screen.

Similarly, our comfort and experiences in the journey of life will depend on how well we follow the instructions in God's word. This point is possibly where many Christians fall short. Many Christians pray and read the word of God but they do not obey it. The manifestation of God's power is not just in the studying or the declaration of the word of God but in applying it. The power in the word renews and transforms our lives. God's word will make a success out of any person who dares to obey it.

Don't just read the Bible and forget about it afterwards. Read it regularly and let the word of God sink into your heart. Remind yourself of the deep spiritual truths daily and let it become a part of you to take hold of your inheritance. Apostle James cautioned us:

> But don't just listen to God's word. You must do what it says. Otherwise, you are only fooling yourselves. For if you listen to the word and don't obey, it is like glancing at your face in a mirror. You see yourself, walk away, and forget what you look like. But if you look carefully into the perfect law that sets you free, and if you do what it says and don't forget what you heard, then God will bless you for doing it. (James 1:22-25 NLT)

Everything we need to enjoy a prosperous life in Christ Jesus is already prepared for us. Apply God's word and take hold of it. From the first book of the Bible, Genesis, up until the last book, Revelation, God has always emphasised obedience and the blessings that come with it. Walking in obedience to God releases God's blessing in our lives (Deuteronomy 28:1-14).

Let's look at some scriptures on obedience below:

> If you carefully obey me and are faithful to the terms of my promise, then out of all the nations you will be my own special possession, even though the whole world is mine. (Exodus 19:5 GW)

> "Now if you faithfully obey the Lord your God and are careful to follow all his commands I am giving you today, the Lord your God will put you far above all the nations of the earth. All these blessings will come and overtake you, because you obey the Lord your God: (Deuteronomy 28:1-2 CSB)

> "If you love me, you will keep my commandments. (John 14:15)

> And God gives us what we ask for. We receive it because we obey God's commands and do what pleases him. (1 John 3:22 GW)

> "Look, I am coming soon! Blessed are those who obey the words of prophecy written in this book."
> (Revelation 22:7 NLT)

Warning against partial obedience

Partial obedience is one of the greatest enemies of Christians today. By partial obedience, I mean when we pick and choose what to obey in God's word. Partial obedience gives us this false sense of "I'm trying" mindset or we say, "but other people are doing worse things." We ought to compare ourselves to God's word not other people. What God says is wrong, is wrong and that should be the end of the matter. Our opinions don't change what God has said. When God says something is not right, even if most people engage in it, it's still not right.

There are some Christians who have two different lifestyles. They want the best of God and the best of the world. They want God's approval but also want the world's approval. They live compromising lives and do things to please themselves. They have ignored God's standards and have set their own standards.

There are Christians who are happy to turn up to church but won't stop having sex outside of marriage. There are some Christians who are happy to come to church but won't forgive. There are some Christians who'll give but won't forgive. There are some who will leave the rave on Saturday night and sing in the choir on Sunday morning. There are some Christians who will worship God but will also worship the devil through secular songs. There are some Christians who wear revealing clothes and put half naked pictures of themselves on social media and then claim to "rep" God.

The truth is that if we live double lives we won't have any real testimonies. We'll also struggle to locate the winning word we need to live a victorious life. The Holy Spirit helps us to locate the winning word in the Bible that will give us victory over our trials. However, we grieve the Spirit when we live a sinful lifestyle (Ephesians 4:30), and we become less sensitive to Him. As a result, it becomes more difficult to detect His leadings and promptings. Also, when we live in sin God won't answer our prayers (Psalm 66:18).

We need to pray for greater infilling of the Holy Spirit to overcome every sin we consistently fall into.

Partial obedience and the tragic end of King Saul

It is important to understand that partial obedience is disobedience. Disobedience carries consequences just like any other life choices. Sometimes it can have a lasting effect on your life just like King Saul.

The story of King Saul is one of the saddest stories in the Bible (Read 1 Samuel chapters 10 to 31). He went from being God's choice into being God's reject because of partial obedience. Remember that partial obedience is when we pick and choose what to obey in God's word. You should take time and examine his life but for the purpose of this book I will focus on 1 Samuel chapter 15 because this is where we see the miserable consequences of a Christian who chooses to live a life of partial obedience. God's instructions to King Saul was to completely destroy all the Amalekites and not spare any person or animal,

Now go and attack Amalek, and utterly destroy all that they have, and do not spare them. But kill both man and woman, infant and nursing child, ox and sheep, camel and donkey.'" (1 Samuel 15:3)

Saul carried out the assignment but he didn't do everything God asked him to do. Saul spared the King of the Amalekites and some animals,

> But Saul and the people spared Agag and the best of the sheep, the oxen, the fatlings, the lambs, and all that was good, and were unwilling to utterly destroy them. But everything despised and worthless, that they utterly destroyed. (1 Samuel 15:9)

Saul justified his partial obedience when Prophet Samuel confronted him about sparing some animals. Saul had opportunities to repent but he justified his actions and blamed other people. Let us see some of his excuses:

> And Saul said, "They have brought them from the Amalekites; for the people spared the best of the sheep and the oxen, to sacrifice to the Lord your God; and the rest we have utterly destroyed." (1 Samuel 15:15)

And again,

> And Saul said to Samuel, "But I have obeyed the voice of the Lord, and gone on the mission on which the Lord sent me, and brought back Agag king of Amalek; I have utterly destroyed the Amalekites. But the people took of the plunder, sheep and oxen, the best of the things which should have been utterly destroyed, to sacrifice to the Lord your God in Gilgal." (1 Samuel 15:20-21)

The reason why God told Saul to destroy all the Amalekites was because they were a symbol of sin. In effect God was saying destroy every sin. But Saul only destroyed some sins.

The author of Hebrews warns us to get rid of every sin in our lives,

We have all these great people around us as examples. Their lives tell us what faith means. So we, too, should run the race that is before us and never quit. We should remove from our lives anything that would slow us down and the sin that so often makes us fall. (Hebrews 12:1)

This wasn't King Saul's only blip. He had previously made an unlawful sacrifice (1 Samuel 13) and also had hatred in his heart towards David (1 Samuel 18:29). Although King Saul did some good things for God, he was inconsistent and didn't repent of his actions as we saw earlier. This was just another step in King Saul's life of partial obedience. The result was God's judgment:

> So Samuel said: "Has the Lord as great delight in burnt offerings and sacrifices, As in obeying the voice of the Lord? Behold, to obey is better than sacrifice, And to heed than the fat of rams. For rebellion is as the sin of witchcraft, And stubbornness is as iniquity and idolatry. Because you have rejected the word of the Lord, He also has rejected you from being king." (1 Samuel 15:22-23)

In the end, God rejected Saul as a King. God demonstrated that He desires complete obedience above anything else. Our offerings and church attendance are good but He wants us to fully obey Him. When we fully obey God, we'll experience His fullness. But if we disobey God, it means we're rejecting Him and He will also reject us. Therefore Jesus said,

> "Not everyone who says to me, 'Lord, Lord!' will enter the kingdom of heaven, but only the person who does what my Father in heaven wants. Many will say to me on that day, 'Lord, Lord, didn't we prophesy in your name? Didn't we force out demons and do many miracles by the power and authority of your name?' Then I will tell them publicly, 'I've never known you. Get away from me, you evil people.' (Matthew 7:21-23 GW)

Although this scripture above is talking about false prophets, I believe that it applies to all of us because God is not a respecter of persons. The word of God applies to everyone. We need to reject partial obedience and live in complete obedience to God at all times.

The story of King Saul is one that I can relate to but on a significantly less serious scale. I used to work as a customer assistant in a cinema when I was in sixth form. It was during the summer holidays and on my way to work one day, the Holy Spirit prompted me to go on a three days fast. But I reasoned to myself that I didn't need to fast because I didn't have any major needs and everyone in my family was okay. Rather than the 3 days God instructed, I decided to fast for a day in case something bad was about to happen. I fasted just one day from 6am to 6pm.

Now on what would have been my second day of the fast, a customer came to buy nachos and a drink, but he changed his mind. Now those who work or have worked in the cinema know that when a customer changes their mind after they've been served, we just throw the food away. But on this occasion, I was going on my break shortly so I decided not to throw the food away and enjoy it during my break. After all, it was going to be wasted in the bin. Now I went upstairs to the break room where we usually went to take our breaks. While I was busy tucking into the nachos, a manager came in and asked me if I paid for it and I responded no. On another day, any other manager would have turned a blind eye or given me a casual telling off. It had happened with others before.

However, this lady escalated the issue and managed to get me suspended. She even pushed for a criminal record. When I realised the seriousness of the case, I had to fast and pray to God for forgiveness and for Him to stop the criminal record, as that would seriously affect my employment opportunities. God answered my prayer and when I went for a meeting with the managers, they stated that they had dropped the criminal charges because of my good record as an employee.

This story shows that partial obedience can have serious ramifications for Christians. Don't pick and choose what to obey but be fully obedient. If you want God to be fully involved in your affairs then do exactly what He tells you to do. Walking in full obedience to God and doing His will, ensures that you fulfil your glorious destiny in Jesus Christ. Don't give in to the pressures of the world so that you can enjoy the pleasures in the Kingdom.

REPENTANCE

The word repentance is not just saying, "I'm sorry". It means having a change of mind, which results in a change of action. In other words, you'll know if you're truly sorry for something when you stop doing it. It's true that nobody is perfect and we all make mistakes but God doesn't want us to live in sin. He expects us to come to Him and ask for forgiveness and then change our actions. Apostle John said that,

God is faithful and reliable. If we confess our sins, he forgives them and cleanses us from everything we've done wrong. (1 John 1:9 GW)
If the offence is also against other people, then we should also go to them and ask for their forgiveness.

FINAL REMARKS

As you obey the word of God and apply the principles in this book, you'll always locate the right word. Locating and obeying the right word or the winning word will enable us to overcome life's challenges and live a victorious life. I see you rising to the top and influencing your world in Jesus name!

SALVATION PRAYER

The principles taught in this book will only work for you if you accept Jesus as your Lord and Saviour. You can only discover and enjoy the winning word when you accept Jesus into your heart and have His blood cleanse your sins. If you want to accept Jesus as your Lord and Saviour, please say the following prayer from the depth of your heart:

> Lord Jesus,
> I believe that you died for me.
> And on the third day you rose again.
> Please forgive me my sins and cleanse me with your blood.
> Come into my life now, Lord.
> Come into my heart and be my king, my Lord, and my Saviour.
> From today, I will no longer live for myself and be controlled by sin but I will follow you all the days of my life.
> So help me God.
> In Jesus mighty name I pray. Amen!

Congratulations! You're now a child of God. Please find a Bible believing church and join them in fellowship. A church is an important part of the Christian journey because you go there to learn more about God. You will also meet other Christians who will encourage and help you in your Christian journey.

If this is the first time you have made the decision to accept Jesus into your heart, drop me an email at: michael_osei@hotmail.com to receive a free copy of the Bible. Your life will never be the same!

Chapter Notes

Printed in Poland
by Amazon Fulfillment
Poland Sp. z o.o., Wrocław